HUMANKIND

I0409805

THE

CUSTODIANS

OF

WEALTH

OLAKUNBI IJISHAKIN

HUMANKIND THE CUSTODIANS OF WEALTH

© 2022 Publishing
1ª edition

Contents

DEDICATION

I dedicate this book to my Lord Jesus Christ, the Author and Finisher of my faith, the Holy Spirit of God who guided me with the living and infallible Word of God. Thanking the following for their care and support at all times; my Family members, In-laws, Friends & co. Pastors, the Church Family. Most especially my late parents, husband, and senior ones.

My life journey has been from glory to glory, despite all odds since I gave my life to God, The Lord Jesus Christ has been the only source and strength of my life.

Finally, my special thanks to God for my wonderful children - Christina, Emmanuel, and David. I will forever be grateful for your devotion to the Almighty God. God bless you all.

PREFACE

This book is intended to create an awareness of how wealthy the human race is, and to explore diverse areas available for you to flourish, focusing particularly on monetary wealth. Human beings are carriers of treasures and have astonishing unique traits. For example when you conduct a 'DNA', it is only uniquely linked to an individual, this makes every human being the wealthiest being and very rare among all kinds on the planet, to the extent that we are the custodians of the whole planet world!

As a person, it is key for you to manage every resource you are naturally enriched with. This book highlights the importance of money, being a good custodian of wealth, and many valuable insights.

I desire to enrich the next generation with wealthy and informed knowledge and empower this generation to leave an inheritance to the coming generation accordingly.

CHAPTER ONE

CHAPTER ONE

Custodian of Riches
PRACTICE THE 50 / 30 / 20 RULES

CHAPTER ONE

Custodian of riches

Custodians

Custodians can be explained, as the persons who hold responsibility to watch over important, expensive assets in the closet.

A person entrusted with guarding or maintaining a property; care taker. (thefreedictionary.com) Dictionary Definition:

Every human being has a root, and the root can be traced to a family tree many years back. The human race lineage has been equipped with their peculiar wealth and riches 'If sound researches are conducted, you will find the unique wealth in that lineage'

Nature itself is an advantage of wealth to humans and it's for us to improve, therefore – global warming needs to be addressed to ensure that the world moves in the right positive direction. Everyone can be educated in this area so that the rich nature will yield benefits and not the alarming news that we are encountering now.

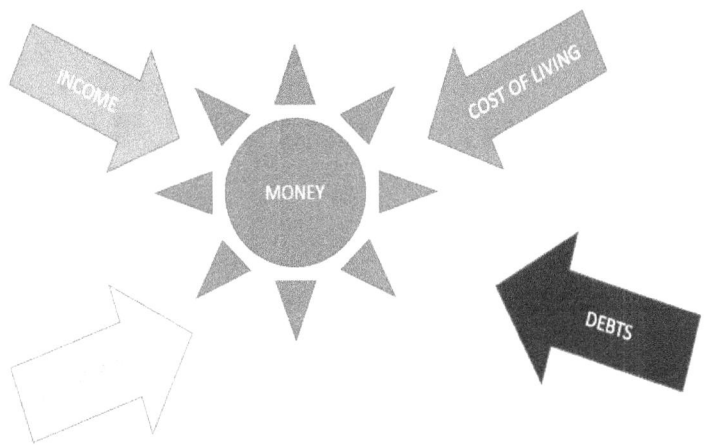

More countries would have been better off economically if their resources were channelled toward research and development. The wealth in many nations is yet to be discovered; unfortunately, the ones that have discovered their nation's wealth are mismanaging their wealth. Most citizens of some nations are potential millionaires! Disappointingly the wealthy custodians of wealth in the world are more dependent on other humans for wealth, and living in limitation. 'Meaning we have many poor people who are naturally rich', but they do not have access to wealth and now, have to depend on the rich in our nations.

For example, a nation that is wealthy in technology development should find a means to ensure that the majority of the citizens are equipped. Also, a nation rich in agriculture should channel its energy toward farming, etc.

Having mentioned, a nation should equip the citizens, then it's also the responsibility of an individual to be mindful of what is evolving in their environment, and take advantage to generate wealth.

The wealth generated can be likened to wealth within one's custody. Although you have access to all the wealth, and riches at your disposal to spend, save, and pass on to the next generation – I humbly submit that the human race is still custodian – as we brought nothing to this world and we won't take anything beyond □

However we all need to live comfortably, therefore it is important to acquire an understanding of how and what in terms of money; making money and spending and saving is part of the areas covered in this book.

HUMANKIND THE CUSTODIANS OF WEALTH

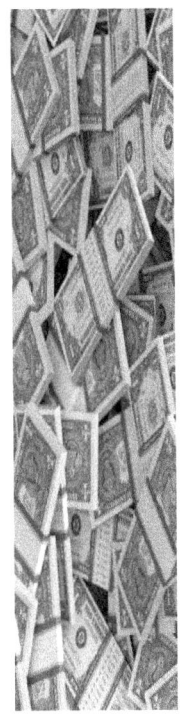

Practice the 50/30/20 rules. The % of Your Money shared is as follows:

50	30	20
The Essential /NEEDS	WANTS	SAVINGS & Investment and clear off Debts

PRACTICE THE 50 / 30 / 20 RULES

Share your income to a percentage

50%: Apportion towards the Essential

30%: Apportion towards Wants

20%: Apportion towards Savings Investments, and pay off Debt

SUMMARY OF CHAPTER ONE

This is an activity section for you to write out the summary of what you have learned from chapter one

For example: one of the summary lessons is that my unique skills may likely, be linked to my family lineage.

<u>PERSONAL ACTION POINT IN CHAPTER ONE</u>

In this section, you can note down the necessary actions you'd take from the highlights in chapter one

NOTES	ACTIONS

For example:

Notes – Manage my income

Actions – I will put a percentage ratio around my income.

HUMANKIND THE CUSTODIANS OF WEALTH
<u>AVAILABLE SUPPORTS IN CHAPTER ONE</u>

In this section, you can note down the required support to help improve your action plans noted in chapter one

<u>NOTES</u>	<u>SUPPORTS</u>

For example:

Notes – Manage my income

Supports – I will liaise with financial experts in other to review my spending habits.

CHAPTER TWO

CHAPTER TWO

Access to Hidden Wealth

Areas to Embrace in other to have access to the hidden wealth's

REVEALING A FEW HIDDEN TREASURES
SEVEN ACCESSIBLE WEALTH

CHAPTER TWO

Every nation and generation has one or many hidden wealth, it influences the people living in the country individually, or collectively. The resources of wealth within a country impact you directly or indirectly, and the circle keeps going on to generations – for example, a wealthy environment will have traits of diverse innovative ideas and solutions; in my current generation, it's the computer age whereby it has predominantly taken over and cut across all business sectors and transform how we relate and interacts as human, anyone cut-off in-between will not have access to the hidden wealth. Of course, computers have been in existence for many years, however, the current generation is now pushing towards 'Artificial Intelligence - AI' and the future generation will definitely diversify to improve the current trend, so anyone eagerly seeking to access the hidden wealth needs to learn fast!

YOU ARE NATURALLY GIFTED AS AN INDIVIDUAL - EQUIPPED WITH UNIQUE DIVERSE WEALTH

Areas to Embrace in other to have access to the hidden wealth's

MONEY IS IMPORTANT!

- **Be a fast learner:** Keep abreast with the innovations
- .
- **Embrace changes:** Change is a constant thing in life and we need to welcome it when it occurs.
- **Tackle Challenges as opportunities:** When you are faced with difficulties **be determined to find a solution, 'prayerfully', and see it as an avenue to many open doors.**
- **Positive mindset:** To access the hidden wealth, it is important to have a positive attitude and take a step-by-step approach when the treasures are in process, and when the treasures have been found.
- **Search inward:** Personal self-review and be devoted towards self-development. Spend Time - Alone

REVEALING A FEW HIDDEN TREASURES

INTERNET:

As the current generation has embraced technology; Whatever area of job or work of your interest – should have an internet impact. Many free online tools can teach you how to use the internet, and you can also approach someone to train you; self-taught is the most popular way - many people have learned the basic areas such as creating content, awareness of using the popular websites, apps, and other important internet tools is a must for this generation if you aim to have a lasting job and enjoy your work.

AFFILIATES:

Another means is finding a company that you can associate with and they will pay you for advertising their services. For Example; if you are someone who enjoys reading – you can get paid for the articles you read and reviewed (A) There are lots of websites paying if you read and review (B) Affiliates If you enjoy shopping, you <u>may need your own space for this</u> 'you can approach companies that you buy products from to be their affiliates "I won't recommend names'
- Use the Search Engine, and view 'affiliates' you will be able to find some of the ones that are among your interests, to get paid for doing what you like best!

CREATIVITY:

There is a unique selling code for you in your creativity. For example, if we engage the ten most talented musicians, even if they are requested to put the same song together, they will all shine in their respective ways. I would like to encourage you to continue to improve your creativity and find means to showcase your work.

- **Be a fast learner:** Keep abreast with the new innovations.

- **Embrace changes:** Change is a constant thing in life, and we need to welcome it when it occurs.

- **Search inward:** Personal self-review and be devoted towards self-development. Spend Time - Alone

SEVEN ACCESSIBLE WEALTH

The seven accessible wealth mentioned here in this book, are very popular, however your attitudes towards them matter; each one of them can either create wealth or remain dormant in your life, as they remain with you continuously!

(1) **The Creator**: Every mankind has access to the creator of the universe, and the blessings in Him

(2) **Lineage / People:** 'manpower' the synergy of people around us is a blessing - either (family & friends/associates, work colleagues, church, etc)

(3) **Health:** The popular saying; that health is wealth, remains factual.

(4) **Time:** Time spent well, can be equalised to money invested well; as time is money.

(5) **Money:** Money remains powerful, and how you manage the little or a lot in your possession matters - this book will focus mostly on money management and wealth.

(6) **Skills /Talent/ Knowledge:** You remain unique in this area.

(7) **Inhabitant of the Universe:** The world and the inhabitant have a role to play in the life of humanity, every discovery from the universal, that you are

interested in, if you do further research and development - is accessible for you to create wealth.

REFLECTION

SUMMARY OF CHAPTER TWO

This is an activity section for you to write out the summary of what you have learned from chapter two

For example one of the summary lessons is that I can use my space to link with other companies in other to earn extra income through an affiliate program

PERSONAL ACTION POINT IN CHAPTER TWO

In this section, you can note down the necessary actions you'd take from the highlights in chapter two

NOTES	ACTIONS

For example:

Notes – Fast Learner

Actions – I will be open and keen to learn new skills in other to be ahead always in my area of expertise.

AVAILABLE SUPPORTS IN CHAPTER TWO

In this section, you can note down the required support to help improve your action plans noted in chapter two

NOTES	SUPPORTS

For example:

Notes – Fast Learner

Supports – I may need to attend short courses online.

CHAPTER THREE

CHAPTER THREE

Financial Intelligence
MONEY AS CURRENCY
Practice the 50/30/20 rules
Healthy money management system

CHAPTER THREE

Financial Intelligence

It is important to be equipped with adequate Wisdom and Support on How to MANAGE YOUR MONEY Regularly, by effectively documenting your finances and keeping track of it, will make a lot of difference!

MONEY AS CURRENCY

You can liken money to a currency of light that flows from a source, and as It flows in and out, the more inflow you have the better for you!

Examples of inflow

- Salary is the most popular inflow
- Content creator 'YouTube monetizing' TikTok, Facebook, etc
- Selling items or talent is another means of inflow 'write book' 'entertainment' bake' cook, be a tutor, etc
- Affiliate marketing: Linking up with diverse companies can improve your income later on, or

immediately "example: advertise products for a business or someone.

- Recycle old items – don't throw them away! sell them
- Rent unused space in the house 'garage' car 'rent out for filming or short-term stay.
- It can also be a non-monetary act: It can be a gift received, in-kind which you can turn into money.
- Showing a kind gesture to humanity, it's simple but it is the truth! 'whatever goes around comes around!
- Saving Financial - Investment can be viewed as a good means of keeping money aside, then yielding interest
- Invest in the property market, and fixed assets wisely, and carefully as some of the investments come with their own risk, so it's better to be familiar with any platform you would want to invest in and learn how to invest in an unknown market/business: 'stock, cryptocurrency, bonds, etc
- Crowdfunding – this is joining money with other investors then it will realise better returns as the business generates income
- Own your own business – receive a dividend.

HUMANKIND THE CUSTODIANS OF WEALTH

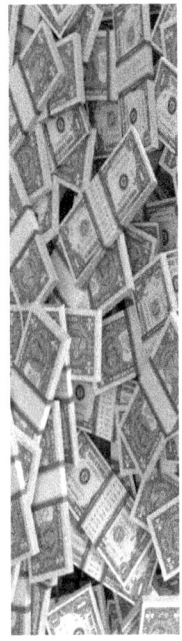

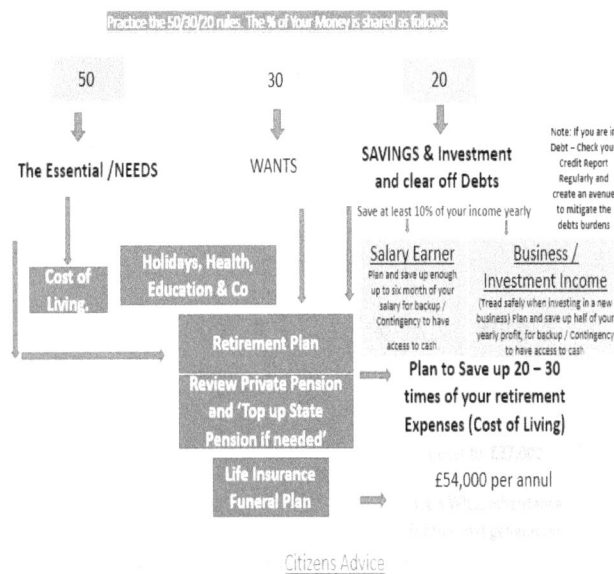

Practice the 50/30/20 rules. The % of Your Money is shared as follows:

50	30	20

The Essential /NEEDS — **WANTS** — **SAVINGS & Investment and clear off Debts**

Save at least 10% of your income yearly

Note: If you are in Debt – Check your Credit Report Regularly and create an avenue to mitigate the debts burdens

Cost of Living.

Holidays, Health, Education & Co

Salary Earner — Plan and save up enough up to six month of your salary for backup / Contingency to have access to cash

Business / Investment Income — (Tread safely when investing in a new business) Plan and save up half of your yearly profit, for backup / Contingency to have access to cash

Retirement Plan

Review Private Pension and 'Top up State Pension if needed'

Plan to Save up 20 – 30 times of your retirement Expenses (Cost of Living)

Life Insurance Funeral Plan

£54,000 per annul

Citizens Advice

Practice the 50/30/20 rules. The % of Your Money is shared as follows

20%: SAVINGS & Investment and clear off Debts:

Save at least 10% of your income yearly

Note: If you are in Debt – Check your Credit Report Regularly and create an avenue to mitigate the debt burdens

Salary Earner Plan and save up enough up to six months of your salary for backup / Contingency to have access to cash

Business / Investment Income (Tread safely when investing in a new business) Plan and save up half of your yearly profit, for backup / Contingency to have access to cash

50%: The Essential /NEEDS

Cost of Living:

Also, some of the essentials fall within the wants

Holidays, Health, Education & Co

30%: WANTS

Retirement Plan

Review Private Pension and 'Top up State Pension if needed'

HUMANKIND THE CUSTODIANS OF WEALTH
Life Insurance, Funeral Plan

Live a WILL, inheritance for the next generation

Plan to Save up to 20 – 30 times of your retirement Expenses (Cost of Living)

closer to £27,000 to £54,000 per annul

Get free advice from (Citizens Advice U.K.)

Examples of out-flow

- **Spending on living expenses: Rent, Mortgages, Utility bills, Food, children's needs, Transportation, clothing, etc.**
- **Spending now, for future Impact: Educating yourself, your children, or sponsoring someone else - any cost related to these, are good as they are**

HUMANKIND THE CUSTODIANS OF WEALTH
meant for life improvement, for future
development purposes.

- Investment: Cash bond, ISAS, Deposit Savings.
- life insurance, health, home insurance, etc
- Charity support/donation
- Recreational, holiday, health, and wellbeing
- Careless spending: Anything that goes towards
  wasteful manners or habits should be avoided.

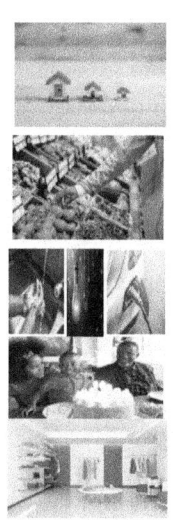

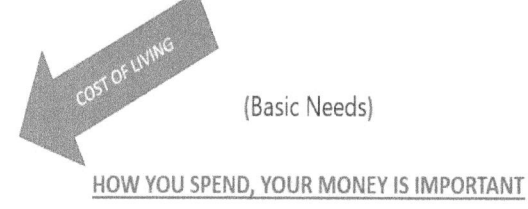

(Basic Needs)

HOW YOU SPEND, YOUR MONEY IS IMPORTANT

DON'T SPEND UNWISELY

PICK YOUR OPTIONS WISELY

Managing the abundance that is in your care and that which you are opportune to have around you is vital!

BUDGETING

You can liken money to a currency of light that flows from a source, and as It flows in and out, the more inflow you have the better for you!

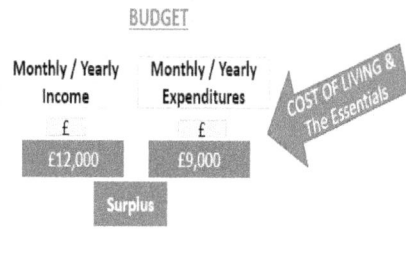

Acknowledging, where the money will be coming from, and what it will be spent on is the key picture for any budget.

- Plan a budget: Writing down all avenues of inflow and outflow in each of the budget's lines is the first step to managing your money.
- Budget for one-off expenses. Some expenses only happen occasionally, such as Christmas, Anniversaries, and also contingency plans.

Whilst the budget has been put together, it will provide ways to mitigate against "debts"

DEBTS

HUMANKIND THE CUSTODIANS OF WEALTH

It is advisable to find ways to increase one's income, through 'multiple income streams' and live within one's inflow, rather than borrowing, as any money <u>borrowed will become a liability.</u> <u>'Living within your means is the best way to be debt-free!</u>

- Of course, some debt can be seen as a good option, and unavoidable – such as student loans, and mortgages, as they are investments towards the future and will yield returns.'
- Mortgages on properties for instance will yield equity and will increase in value after some years.
- Student finance can be repaid gradually, after the completion of one's education, and you have started working.

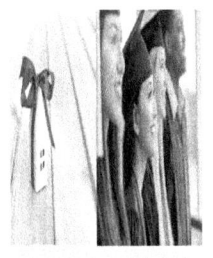

Of course, some debts may be considered as a beneficial option, and unavoidable

- Mortgages on properties for instance will yield equity and will increase in value after some years.
- Student finance can be repaid back gradually, after the completion of one's education, and you have started working.

Avoiding debt such as credit cards and bank loans, 'they are tempting and tend to have higher interest to pay back ' If there is an urgent need', you may request for bank overdraft with lower interest and make it a short-term request.

Student Finance Alternative

- Apprenticeship
- Grants
- Scholarship / Bursaries
- Check under your local council if your borough is committed to supporting (some local council bursaries and grants)
- Your Employer may provide support
- Part-Time Student - Working alongside
- Community funding / (friends, family, well-wishers support)

Some of Credit Card may provide the following incentive

0%
Money/cash back cards
Rewards cards

"Better Still find what you can turn into money; sell unused items, old gifts, share room apartment, etc."

Whilst the budget has been put together, it will provide ways to mitigate against "debts".

It is advisable to find ways to increase one's income, through 'multiple income streams' and live within one's inflow, rather than borrowing, as any money <u>borrowed will become a liability</u>. '<u>Living within your means is the best way to be debt free!</u>

<u>Healthy money management system</u>

I will emphasise that people should have a healthy attitude towards saving money 'There is a popular saying - little drops of water make the mighty ocean'.

If you are in desperate need - Review the need and ensure that you can raise the money through a legitimate means – 'You can write compelling details on <u>GoFundMe</u>' or similar sites, for example towards paying for your education, health issues, unprecedented cost, etc.

- You can also approach other institutions, such as charities, the government, utility companies, etc.

39

Also monitor your bank account regularly, for any strange unplanned spending, to keep track of a healthy money management system. Most people are in a system where cash is not that popular so there is the temptation that you will spend more than what you have in the bank account, Therefore Keep track ahead, by writing down and reviewing your budget regularly, and plan before you spend! 'If it is not necessary to buy it - keep your money!

HOW YOU MAKE MONEY IS IMPORTANT

WORKING HARD PAYS - Although it may be a gradual wealth build; however, it will increase, and last for the future generation to inherit

Here are Clues to Other Popular Ways of Making Money:

- Affiliates advertisements

- Monetising created work

- Crowdfunding / Fundraising for projects – business /UK Gov Small Business Schemes /CIC

Remember life becomes meaningful and beautiful when we know what is happening in the areas of our finances. it's important to keep on top of money issues, work towards how to eliminate debts that tend to cause stress, and move towards healthy money management.

WORKING HARD PAYS - Although it may be a gradual wealth build, however, it will increase and last for the future generation to inherit

Here are Clues to Other Popular Ways of Making Money:

- **Affiliates advertisements**
- **Monetising created work**
- **Crowdfunding / Fundraising for projects - business**

CONSIDER NOT SPENDING RECKLESSLY 'PICK YOUR OPTIONS WISELY'

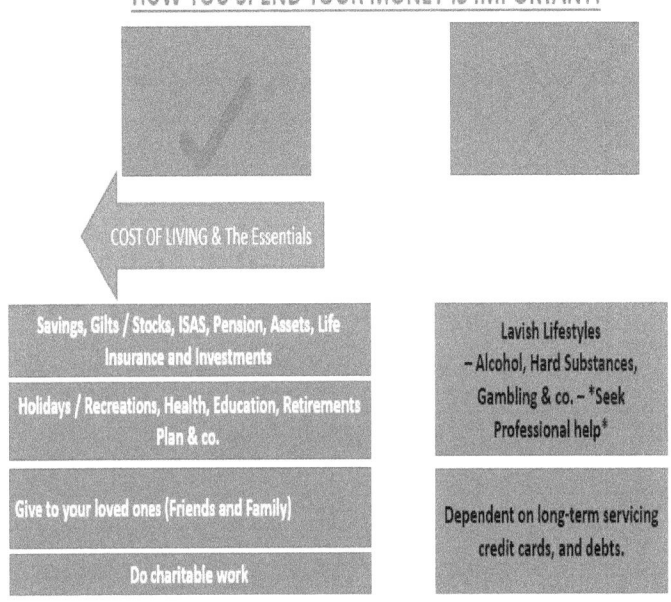

HOW YOU SPEND YOUR MONEY IS IMPORTANT!

COST OF LIVING & The Essentials

Savings, Gilts / Stocks, ISAS, Pension, Assets, Life Insurance and Investments

Holidays / Recreations, Health, Education, Retirements Plan & co.

Give to your loved ones (Friends and Family)

Do charitable work

Lavish Lifestyles – Alcohol, Hard Substances, Gambling & co. – *Seek Professional help*

Dependent on long-term servicing credit cards, and debts.

HUMANKIND THE CUSTODIANS OF WEALTH
CONSIDER SPENDING ON THE FOLLOWING!

COST OF LIVING & The Essentials

Savings, Gilts / Stocks, ISAS, Pension, Assets, Life Insurance, and Investments

Holidays / Recreations, Health, Education, Retirements Plan & Co.

Give your loved ones, Friends, and Family.

Do charitable work

CONSIDER NOT TO SPEND ON THE FOLLOWING

Lavish Lifestyles

– Alcohol, Hard Substances, Gambling & Co. – *Seek Professional help

Dependent on long-term servicing credit cards, and debts.

DON'T BE TOO HARD ON YOURSELF EITHER □

REFLECTION

SUMMARY OF CHAPTER THREE

This is an activity section for you to write out the summary of what you have learned from chapter three

For example: one of the summary lessons is that healthy money management is key and important, as it will protect my wealth.

PERSONAL ACTION POINT IN CHAPTER THREE

In this section, you can note down the necessary actions you'd take from the highlights in chapter three

NOTES	ACTIONS

For example:

Notes – Healthy Money Management

Actions – I will adjust some of the areas I have been spending my money on.

AVAILABLE SUPPORTS IN CHAPTER THREE

In this section, you can note down the required support to help improve your action plans noted in chapter three

NOTES	SUPPORTS

For example:

Notes – Healthy Money Management

Supports – I may have to consider cutting my coat according to my clothes, perhaps cutting my clothes according to my size.

CHAPTER FOUR

CHAPTER FOUR

The Three Diamonds - 'D'

CHAPTER FOUR

The Three Diamonds - 'D'

Firstly, Diamonds used in this content represent a well sort after and rare human being

The dictionary explains diamond: as a precious stone consisting of a clear and colourless crystalline form of pure carbon, the hardest naturally occurring substance. (lexico.com/definition)

Listed here are 'D' for Diamond: You as a unique human being, you are worth more than millions of diamonds, you are indeed precious, and wealthy in your uniqueness. However, to make it easy to remember - I have used the following words, and explained each of the words below:

D – Delivered Diamond:

D – Discovered Diamond:

D – Developed Diamond:

D – Delivered Diamond

This is in my own words, apart from the academic educational skills; there are diverse activities you do day to day - naturally and effortlessly without noticing that you are actively engaging in the practice daily, and yearly respectively. For example, I enjoy humming around and singing. At some point in time, people started encouraging me to set up my music band, produce an album, etc. We all have that built-in talent in us – Another example is a friend of mine who enjoys baking cake, back then in secondary school - she is now an amazing baker.

D – Discovered Diamond

Every human being tends to stumble into this stage of undiscovered talent, and later on discover a silent, 'unnoticed talent that will 'wow the world'.

I will use myself as an example again, being good and more interested in mathematics at school then, also working closely with my mother to calculate her trade profits, I was not keen on the English language/literature, although I do get encouraged by my father to write him letters which he reviews frequently, as times pass by, I developed interest, and enjoy writing, from just letters, I moved to notes, articles, and never thought in my wildest dream that I will ever write a book.. 'but here I am.

D – Developed Diamond

This is the stage that no one can outgrow until we leave, the planet world, in a professional setting - It is called 'Continuous Professional Development (CPD), It is a wise idea – if you engage yourself in the habit of learning soft skills, **and new innovation at your own space, and time to keep abreast of your continuous development,** whatever skills either already delivered, discovered, actively working or silent one, needs to be developed and fine-tuned, 'the world we live in revolves and we can not afford to be left behind in creating wealth and showcasing the wealth too.

Every human being is prone to make money naturally, searching for that simple and unique skill, that is peculiar to you is a responsibility you own yourself. Also learning new skills beyond your beautiful **natural talent** will unravel the hidden wealth at your disposal and give you peace of mind.

REFLECTION

SUMMARY OF CHAPTER FOUR

This is an activity section for you to write out the summary of what you have learned from chapter four

For example: one of the summary lessons is that there are still many skills that I have yet to discover.

PERSONAL ACTION POINT IN CHAPTER FOUR

In this section, you can note down the necessary actions you'd take from the highlights in chapter four

NOTES	ACTIONS

For example:

Notes − skills yet to be discovered

Actions − I will test out other areas of my interest.

AVAILABLE SUPPORTS IN CHAPTER FOUR

In this section, you can note down the required support to help improve your action plans noted in chapter four

NOTES	SUPPORTS

For example:

Notes – skills yet to be discovered

Supports – I may have to finetune, and explore diverse areas of interest, and probably seek assistance from other people for them to highlight other skills they have noticed in me.

CHAPTER FIVE

Generational Inheritances

CHAPTER FIVE

Generational Inheritances
INVESTMENTS

CHAPTER FIVE

Generational Inheritances

It's a rare privilege for many in this age and day to imbibe the principle of generational inheritance, because the world has become more selfish. One of the reasons I was keen to write this book is to emphasise more, how important and advantageous it is for wealth and riches to be inherited. The people of our generation should live intentionally wealth disciplined and selflessly; every family tree has one wealth or many wealth that should have been passed on to the next generation. The human race needs to think ahead and create a good base, accessible platform for their upcoming lineage. The legacy of the wealth inherited from one generation, if passed on to another will circle and will enhance the human race to embrace life better!

• Invest in People

• Invest Your Time Wisely

• Invest Your Money Prudently

Teach Your Young Ones, Children
about Money and How to Manage it!

Generation Wealth Should Be Prioritised

INVESTMENTS

Here is a scenario whereby a generational inheritance was passed on to the next generation, compared to the scenario

whereby no -generational inheritance was passed on to the next generation.

<u>Lineage With Generational Inheritance</u>

Comparing the generation that has left riches, wealth, and assets for their generation

- It is like a bridge created to link someone to their journey safely, quicker, and better - for example, within the royal family in the UK, the descendants are privileged to enjoy the lineage wealth, There is an easy continuous bridge and this legacy will continue.
- A strong financial foundation will pave the way for the new custodians of wealth and make their pathway smooth - for example when you live sufficiently, it makes you strong - 'Money is good, and riches can be likened to strength'
- It makes it easy for the generations to continue to impact one another positively and productively - the wealth will increase, and the future inheritance will multiply, to the next generation.

Lineage With No Generational Inheritance

Comparing the generation that has left no riches, wealth, or assets for their generation

- **Most, family trees can be linked to a wealthy person at one time or the other, however, an unfortunate case could have affected the wealth to continue in the same lineage**
- **If there is no generation inheritance, there is a probability for the generation to struggle, even with continuous troubles that can have a negative effect on the lineage.**
- **It may lead to a lack of motivation, as the only focus will be on how to live comfortably for now and not intending to leave an inheritance, as they may keep struggling, and never have enough.**

Generation wealth should be prioritised:

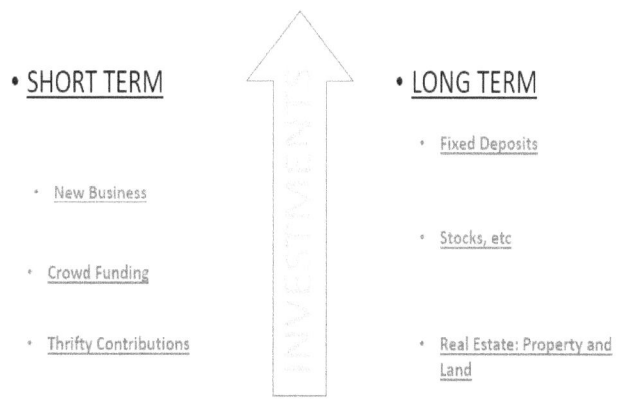

* SHORT TERM

  · New Business

  · Crowd Funding

  · Thrifty Contributions

* LONG TERM

  · Fixed Deposits

  · Stocks, etc

  · Real Estate: Property and Land

INVESTMENTS

- SHORT TERM: New Business, Crowd Funding, Thrifty Contributions

- LONG TERM: Fixed Deposit, Stocks, Real Estate, Property, and Land, etc

HUMANKIND THE CUSTODIANS OF WEALTH

You can start building wealth gradually now, by looking into areas such as real estate property, saving money, crypto, money, investments, stocks, bonds, family businesses, or legitimate means that have monetary value. Start a foundation, either charity work or social enterprise, invest in people, and consider taking out life insurance for people with dependents.

Generational wealth building should be intentional, as there will be a plan in place to follow, and checks and balances when there are challenges, 'it won't cause diversion or loss of focus'.

This generation should seek counsel on how to leave an inheritance for the next generation.; in terms of Money, Riches, Assets, Well-being, Keeping the planet and its inhabitants well, etc.

After the generational wealth has been built, it is very important to document the assets, legally – by writing a WILL.

HUMANKIND THE CUSTODIANS OF WEALTH

Finally, every generation's wealth passed down to lineage will help the foundation of the many unborn generations. Inheritance will create an avenue to empower many people that will benefit from it. My desire is to enrich the next generation and empower them accordingly.

REFLECTION

SUMMARY OF CHAPTER FIVE

This is an activity section for you to write out the summary of what you have learned from chapter five

For example: one of the summary lessons is that generational wealth should be prioritised

PERSONAL ACTION POINT IN CHAPTER FIVE

In this section, you can note down the necessary actions you'd take from the highlights in chapter five

NOTES	ACTIONS

For example:

Notes – A linage with generational wealth

Actions – I will ensure I make every necessary financial preparation for my generation.

AVAILABLE SUPPORTS IN CHAPTER FIVE

In this section, you can note down the required support to help improve your action plans noted in chapter five

NOTES	SUPPORTS

For example:

Notes – A linage with generational wealth

Supports – I will explore investment, stock, etc., and seek expert advice.

OTHER BOOKS BY THE AUTHOR

All the books are available via Amazon Kindle

- <u>Merry Marriage</u>
- <u>Christians The Custodians of Wealth</u>
- <u>Delay is Not Denial</u>
- <u>Love Dries My Tears</u>

OTHER BOOK - RECOMMENDED

Walking With God
by Pastor Tobi Ijishakin